MW00748300

 FriesenPress

Suite 300 - 990 Fort St
Victoria, BC, V8V 3K2
Canada

www.friesenpress.com

Copyright © 2020 by Coleen McAvoy
First Edition — 2020

Illustrated by Veronica Chung, Katelyn Sieb, and the Artists Helping Artists team

No part of this publication may be reproduced in any form, or by any means, electronic or mechanical, including photocopying, recording, or any information browsing, storage, or retrieval system, without permission in writing from the author or FriesenPress.

The biblical information is believed to be factual as recorded in the Bible. All illustrations or analogies are fictitious. Any similarity to real persons, living or dead, is coincidental and not intended by the author or illustrators.

For more information please email: inthebeginning80@gmail.com

To purchase a copy of this book, visit www.friesenpress.com; or Amazon.com

All rights reserved.

ISBN
978-1-5255-7516-7 (Hardcover)
978-1-5255-7517-4 (Paperback)
978-1-5255-7518-1 (eBook)

1. JUVENILE NONFICTION, RELIGION, BIBLE STORIES, OLD TESTAMENT

Distributed to the trade by The Ingram Book Company

Have you ever wondered why the first verse in the Bible tells us that, **"In the beginning God created the heavens and the earth,"** and then the second verse says, **"But the earth became waste and emptiness, and darkness was on the surface of the deep?"**

Genesis 1:1-2a

God's creation of the universe was orderly and without any mistakes. When the angels saw how beautiful the earth was, they were very happy.

It seems strange that God would create the beautiful heavens and earth and then let the earth become waste and emptiness. This short book gives you a few clues to help answer some of your questions and begin to solve this awesome secret.

This is a good book to read with your parents. There is a section at the back of the book that gives you some Bible verses and notes that support what you are reading. All these verses and footnotes have been taken from the Recovery Version of the Bible. If you do not have a copy of this version of the Bible with the notes, please refer to the next page to find out how you can get one.

For a thorough understanding of pages 9-13 and 19-23, where the key verses Genesis 1:1-2a, Isaiah 14:12-15, and Ezekiel 28:12-17 with the notes are extensively used, please refer to the works cited section on page 57.

If you want the Holy Bible Recovery Version (Old and New Testament with the footnotes), you can purchase it online using the following link:
https://www.livingstream.com/en/12-bibles (Hardcover or bonded leather)

To purchase an electronic version:
New Testament Recovery Version of the Bible (with footnotes), https://www.lsm.org/epublications.html select Kindle

Holy Bible Recovery Version (Old and New Testament with footnotes), select iSilo

To receive a free copy of the New Testament Recovery Version of the Bible (with footnotes), please select the appropriate link for your own country:

Australia: https://www.biblesforaustralia.org.au/

Canada: https://www.biblesforcanada.org/order

Countries in Europe: https://www.biblesforeurope.org/

New Zealand: https://www.biblesfornewzealand.org.nz/

United States of America: https://www.biblesforamerica.org/

Table of Contents

THE HIDDEN LINK,

AN AWESOME SECRET

God's Wisdom and Lucifer's Counterfeit in Genesis

A PERSONAL RECOLLECTION

When I was young, my younger brother and I would make a hole in the ground, pile up dirt and stones around its edge, and carefully plant some twigs. Then we would get some buckets of water from the stream which ran through our yard and fill the hole with water. Our little rubber toy animals and people were placed around the lake, and our little boat would float in the water.

We had a problem. During the night, the water in the lake disappeared into the soil. The twigs never turned into trees, the people just sat there doing nothing, and the animals only moved when we moved them.

We also made some discoveries. Although we did not bury any seeds in the dirt, we saw tiny blades of grass growing around our lake. Leafy weeds were springing up all over the place. Hundreds of energetic ants would come to visit, and when we were not looking, the barn swallows would take mud from our lake to make their nests. These things were so full of life.

Even though we put a lot of effort into building that dirt farm, we soon lost interest in it.

Now it was more fun to go exploring. We would go for hikes along the stream. We wondered why the spring at the source of the stream always had big air bubbles coming to the surface. Where did these bubbles come from? Why did the water not freeze, when the weather was really cold? This little spring was the source of not only our drinking water, but also the drinking water for all the animals that lived on our family farm. As we continued to hike along the stream bed, we discovered that there was no water beyond the spring. There were pebbles and sand, small brush, and even grass but the ground was dry. When we hiked as far as the barbed wire fence that marked the end of our father's property, we could see a flat valley with big hills extending for miles but still no water.

IN THE BEGINNING GOD CREATED

We knew this beautiful landscape was created and designed by God. We even called it "God's Country." But we did not really realize that God was taking care of us by providing for our needs in so many secret ways. We enjoyed water from the spring, milk from the cows, fresh eggs from the chickens, fresh vegetables from the garden, and fresh meat from the animals that lived on the farm. When we helped our dad haul bales of hay out to the cattle so they had something to eat when the snow was deep, it never dawned on us that God, a very long time ago, said "Let the earth sprout grass," and that He designed the grass in such a way that year after year it turned green in the spring as soon as the snow melted and the sun shone brightly, and in no time at all it would be tall enough to cut and bale into hay. We took it all for granted.

In eternity past, even before God created the heavens and the earth, God was on the throne above the heavens. In His wisdom He had a plan, a deep desire in His heart. He made the decision to choose man to be His counterpart. Genesis 1:1 records His first step out of eternity into time! This was when He created the heavens and the earth.

God saw the whole earth from His dwelling place above the [1]circle of the earth.

He saw the heavens.

[2]God created the heavens, so He knew what was there from the day He spoke them into being. As He gazed at what He created, He saw the galaxies, [3]the perfect order of the stars, the comets, the big and small meteorites, the moons, the clouds of gases now known as nebulas, and the planets. The moon reflected the light of the sun onto the earth during the night. The beautiful yellow-green, purple-blue, and sometimes red lights were shining and dancing in the atmosphere above the earth. He knew the source of these colorful displays of beauty, and He knew how they came into being. The heavens that He created were colorful, beautiful, and vast. Everything was in perfect order.

He saw the earth.

He saw hills and valleys. Flowing rivers, lakes, and sparkling streams were everywhere. Fish swam in the cool waters. Trees and plants grew along the banks. Birds flew above the water and made their nests in the trees and in the long grass. They were busy eating seeds and insects.

In the forest, He saw trees, moss, mud, even bacteria growing on nurse logs.

Worms, centipedes, ants, and other bugs were busy munching and chewing on pieces of wood and dying plant material. They were hiding under the deep grass, under rocks, fallen leaves, and broken tree branches.

The whole earth was filled with all kinds and sizes of beautiful plants and animals that lived in perfect harmony with each other. They expressed God's wisdom and they enjoyed His special care. Some provided protection for others; others became the food that another animal ate. Some grew very large; others remained very tiny and unseen. Each had its place in the cycle of life. Each had its own unique journey. God's creation was under His divine care.

**He saw what was happening, year after year,
deep inside the earth.**

God saw how the earth's surface was impacted by changes in climate, strong winds, and rushing waters.

When He looked below the earth's surface, He saw thick layers of old plant material and animal deposits squeezed so tight, for such a long time, that they became rocks.

Looking deeper into the crust, He saw that some plants and animals had become fossils embedded in the rock. Fossil fuels such as coal, pockets of liquids which became oil, and natural gases were forming.

He saw that the extreme heat and pressure in the mantle and core of the earth produced constant energy which caused some [4]plates in the earth's crust to shift and collide. This created earthquakes and [5]large cracks in the earth's surface.

In some places, volcanoes with flowing lava and hot springs with steaming water were pushing upwards and outwards.

On a smaller scale, large rocks broke apart, or got so hot that they melted and then cooled off again. Smaller rocks became pebbles in riverbeds or sandy beaches, and some even became dust that blew with the wind into the grass.

There was no clock ticking in heaven recording the number of years that passed by. There were no satellites in the heavens and no camera men on site taking pictures of each event that occurred in the universe and on the earth itself.

During this long period of time, God continued to prepare the earth to be a special place for plants, animals, and people to live. The earth was His focus! No other place in the universe received this kind of attention from God. In God's heart, this was important to Him.

God is wise. [6]He had planned and decided these things before He created the universe. He wanted to reveal these hidden secrets.

GOD'S DWELLING PLACE

In the third heaven, there was a special place where God's throne was. His throne was the highest part in His dwelling place. Only God, not even the angels, knew that this place existed. The part below this throne was called the holy mountain of God. Here, on this high mountain, there was a beautiful [7]garden called Eden. Because God's presence was here, there was divine light, love, righteousness, and holiness. God's glory, His patience, His power, His wisdom, and His might were all expressed. This was God's dwelling place even before the heavens and the earth were created.

It is hard for us to draw a picture of this place. There are only a few verses in the Bible that describe it.

Ezekiel 1:26 – "And above the expanse...
was the likeness of a throne."

Ezekiel 28:13a – "You were in Eden, the garden of God.
Every precious stone was your covering,"

LUCIFER'S SPECIAL INVITATION

We know God created the angels before He created the earth because it says in the Bible that the angels shouted for joy when they saw the beautiful earth God had created.

In the heavens, [8]the angels served Him, obeyed Him and worshipped Him. One of these angels, Lucifer, was invited to the place where God's presence was. Lucifer was an archangel. This was the highest position an angel could have. [9]As the anointed cherub, he covered the ark of God. He was perfect in all his ways, full of wisdom, and beautiful. His covering was precious stones. God allowed him to walk up and down in the midst of the stones of fire upon the holy mountain of God in the garden of God. At a certain point in time, [10]Lucifer had the important responsibility:

**To lead the angels to serve and praise God,
and
to [11]govern the earth which God created.**

Lucifer, who was part of God's creation, saw God's creation. He saw the whole universe. His eyes beheld its vastness, its perfect design, and its beauty. Lucifer was asked to govern, not rule, or claim as his own, the earth which God created.

**Ezekiel 28:14 – "You were the anointed cherub who covered *the Ark*;
indeed I set you, so that you were upon the holy mountain of God;
you walked up and down in the midst of the stones of fire."**

LUCIFER'S ATTITUDE AND ACTIONS

God gave Lucifer a chance to be a part of His plan for the earth but something very bad happened.

Lucifer was not satisfied with being one of God's creatures. Instead of worshipping and serving God, Lucifer's heart was lifted up. Formerly, he was bright, but now his wisdom was corrupted. When God created Lucifer, he was beautiful but now he was proud, and he spoke arrogant words. Instead of obeying God, he conceived his own rebellious plan and decided to do what he wanted to do. Every sentence in his plan said:

[12]I will...I will...I will...I will...I will...

Isaiah 14:12-14 – "How you have fallen from heaven, O Daystar, son of the dawn...But you, you said in your heart: I will ascend to heaven; Above the stars of God I will exalt my throne. And I will sit upon the mount of assembly in the uttermost parts of the north. I will ascend above the heights of the clouds; I will make myself like the Most High."

On that day, unrighteousness was found in him. Lucifer had made his own counterfeit plan. He decided that he would ascend to heaven, exalt his throne above the stars of God, and make himself like the Most High. [13]Lucifer invented rebellion in his own heart.

He did not want God to rule over him anymore,
nor did he want to obey and worship God.

**Lucifer left his evil footprints in the heavens,
and then he began to spread to the earth.**

**Lucifer's counterfeit actions were offending God's
glory and His righteousness.**

God did not create pride, disobedience, or rebellion. The Bible tells us that Lucifer's pride, disobedience, and rebellion was spoken [14]"out of his own *possessions*." It came from within Lucifer,
something he possessed that no other creature possessed. It was very contagious, and soon
some of the angels, possibly one third of them, followed him in his rebellion to overthrow God's
authority. This rebellion began to spread not only in the heavens, but also to the earth.

WE CAN LEARN FROM LUCIFER'S FAILURE

Do you remember a time when your mother asked you to do something? She might have said, "Right after school today, I want you to come home and tidy up your bedroom." There was a moment of silence and a secret question. "Why? My room is just fine."

Off to school you went. That question "why?" took root in your heart. After school, when you entered the front door, your mom was sitting on the couch in the front room. When you saw her, for no reason at all, the same thoughts rose up in you again. This time you said some angry words. Then you let your backpack drop to the floor, and you went to your room, and closed the door.

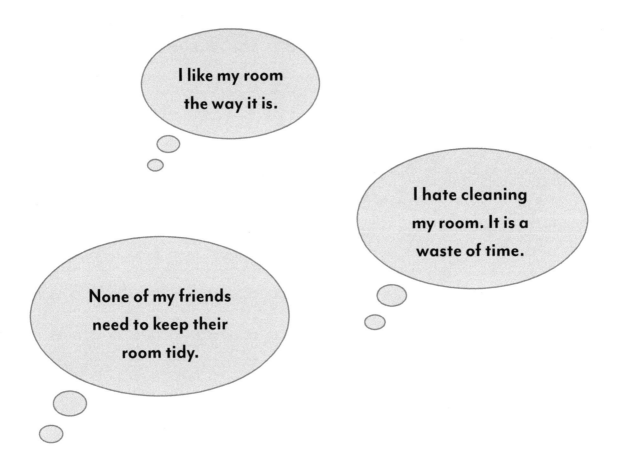

Where did these thoughts and words come from?

They are Lucifer's footprints that want to secretly
sneak into us to contaminate us.

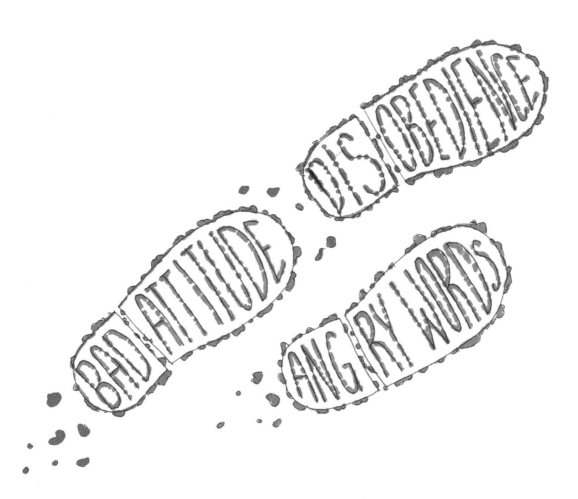

[15]We do not want these footprints to enter our [16]heart.

Proverbs 4:23a – "Keep your heart with all vigilance."

EXAMPLE OF A CALL TO ACTION

Have you ever been a part of a group at school that was working together on a giant project? Imagine your group is growing vegetables. One person is growing a tomato plant; another is growing a watermelon plant. Your part is to grow a sweet potato plant. Every step of the process must be researched and documented. Pictures, either hand-drawn or photos, are essential, and when the time comes to bring your sweet potato fries to class, everyone will want to taste what you grew.

Research begins. You write some entries in your journal.

Your sweet potato tuber is growing small leaves around the top. Tiny white roots are growing around the sides and bottom of the tuber.

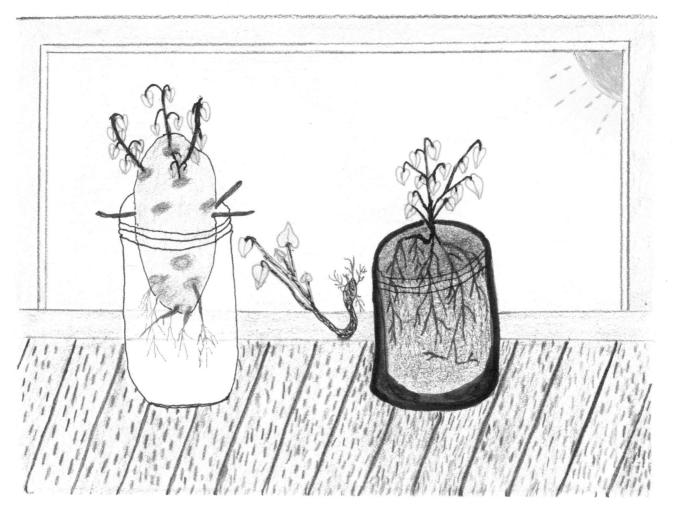

You wait a few weeks and decide to move your sweet potato plant to the garden. You choose the best spot. Every day you inspect it, you water it, and you make entries in your journal. It grows big leaves and begins to spread along the dirt.

One day you notice that a small bug is hiding under a leaf on your plant. It looks like it is chewing into the stem! This could be serious. You go inside and do some research.

It's a sweet potato weevil, and you caught it biting into the stem so that it could lay eggs in the hole. These little eggs were going to go down the inside of the stem into the roots of the plant and eventually make their home in YOUR baby sweet potatoes!

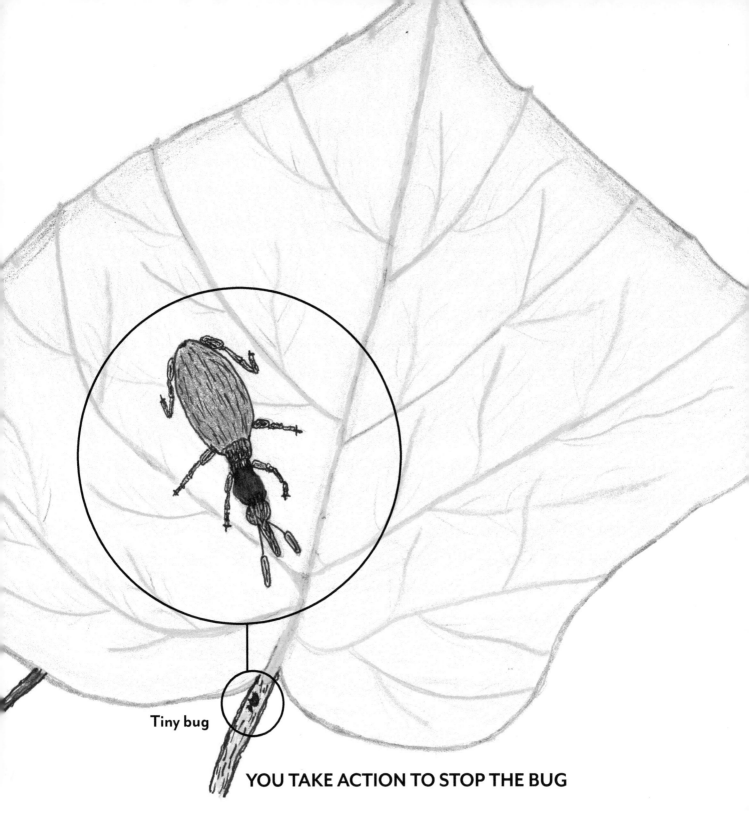

Tiny bug

YOU TAKE ACTION TO STOP THE BUG

You cannot let the bug escape! You quickly collect some sticky duct tape from the drawer, some garden gloves to protect you from getting an insect bite, and your camera for documenting the evidence. You are ready for combat. You cannot let the bug see you coming! Not even one minute can be wasted. Fully equipped and confident, you move in on the culprit and remove it from your plant, carefully putting it on the duct tape. Next step—you take two pictures: one of your bruised plant and one of the weevil. The final step is to carefully fold the duct tape and toss it into the trash can. One bite of your plant is enough!

GOD'S RESPONSE TO LUCIFER'S ACTIONS

As soon as God saw what was growing in Lucifer's heart, He knew that Lucifer was in rebellion and that [17]Lucifer had brought bad footprints to the heavens.

IT WAS TIME FOR GOD TO TAKE ACTION

God judged and sentenced Lucifer, and He [18]cast him out
of His sanctuary. Lucifer was now God's adversary.
His name was changed to "Satan."

The angels who followed Satan in his rebellion were cast out of the heavenlies. They found resting places in the air around the earth and in the sea.

[19]Satan was still allowed to be the ruler of his kingdom, "the kingdom of darkness," and to move about on the earth. However, instead of governing the earth and obeying God, he executed his own counterfeit plan. With the help of the angels who followed him, the earth was brought into a situation that was full of the evil footprints of rebellion and disobedience. Satan had no intention of changing his plan. His goal was to usurp the earth and to claim God's creation for his own purpose.

**God would never allow this to happen.
God's creation belonged to Him, not to Satan.**

IT WAS TIME FOR GOD TO TAKE ACTION AGAIN

Satan's eternal destiny was now determined. God did not judge Satan all at one time. His judgment on Satan is in stages.

It is not known what evil things Satan and the rebellious angels did to the creatures on the earth, and to the earth itself, but we know that it was serious enough to cause God to take action a second time. How long did God wait before He took this step? We do not know. These secrets are still hidden in God's heart. The Bible does tell us that God took Satan's actions very seriously.

RESULT OF GOD TAKING ACTION

Job 9:5-7 – "He who removes mountains, and they do not know it, When He over-turns them in His anger; Who shakes the earth from its place, And its pillars shake; Who commands the sun, and it does not rise, And seals up the stars."

Jeremiah 4:23-24 – "I looked at the earth, and there it was, waste and emp-tiness; And at the heavens, and they had no light. I looked at the mountains, and there they were, shaking, And all the hills were swaying."

Job 38:29-30 – "From whose womb does the ice come forth? And the frost of heaven, who gave birth to it? The waters hide themselves *and become* like stone, And the surface of the deep is frozen."

Psalm 104:6 – "You covered it with the deep as with a garment; The waters stood above the mountains."

[20]To help us understand, God spoke these words to us in the Old Testament.

Archaeologists are discovering places where there are many skeletons of dinosaurs all in one place. They are also finding skeletons of other prehistoric creatures, and petrified fossils of small fish, insects, leaves, ferns, and other plant life. These discoveries are buried under the surface of the earth and found in deserts, rolling hills, valleys, stream beds, and even in mountain ranges. What happened to them, and when did it happen?

Why do some rock formations look like they have a slight tilt to them?

The Mariana trench is very deep. What kind of force did it take to create a trench this deep?

What made the tectonic plates move?

Why did the waters hide themselves and become hard like stone and freeze?

**When and how did all these changes
start to take place?**

**The final answers to all these questions are
hidden in the depths of God's wisdom.**

[21]**Genesis 1:2a – "But the earth became waste and emptiness, and darkness was on the surface of the deep."**

When the angels that were one with God in the heavens looked upon the earth, all they could see was darkness and deep water.

WHERE WAS PLANET EARTH HIDING?

From our point of view, this seems like a very sad picture. From the angels' point of view, it seemed that this was the end of planet Earth.

However, God is wise and loving. [22]He never does anything in a careless or unrighteous way. The original creation was part of His eternal plan. [23]He had no intention of giving up this arrangement or of tossing the earth into the garbage. He already had a plan in place.

[24]God does everything at the right time, even to the exact day. He simply knows what to do, how to do it, and when to do it.

> **Job 42:2 – "I know that You can do all things**
> **and that no purpose of Yours can be restrained."**

Even though big things had happened, [25]the earth never left its place in the solar system. It remained where it was first placed by God. The water on the earth did not run off into other parts of the Milky Way galaxy; it remained on the earth, nor did any piece of the earth float away. The earth did not shatter into pieces. It did not become flat.

Why not? What held it together?

The Bible tells us that God speaks to us in the Son and the Son [26]upholds and bears all things by the word of His power. It also tells us that [27]all things were created in the Son and exist together in Him as the holding center.

Gravity is one example of a force that holds the universe together. Even though we cannot see gravity and we cannot feel it holding us to the earth, we know it is at work. Gravity is a wonderful expression of God's holding power.

Year after year the faithful angels who remained with God
eagerly waited to see what God would do next.

Finally, the time was right.

**GOD BEGAN TO TAKE ACTION AGAIN.
THIS TIME IT WAS TO RESTORE THE EARTH.
HE DID IT IN SIX DAYS.**

While it was still very, very dark,
[28]"the Spirit of God was
brooding upon the surface of the waters."

**In the next few pages,
notice how many times the Bible says:**

[29]"Let...and there was..."

GOD'S WORK TO RESTORE THE EARTH

Day 1
Genesis 1:3–5

"And God said, Let there be light; and there was light." In the evening there was darkness, but in the morning, there was light. **"And God saw that the light was good."**

God, in His wisdom and power, called light back to the earth. The coming of light back to the earth was the beginning of God's work to restore the earth so that living things could again grow and inhabit the earth. The light was hidden behind the darkness, but now it was no longer hidden.

"And God separated the light from the darkness. And God called the light Day, and the darkness He called Night. And there was evening and there was morning, one day." The evening came first and then the morning. There was within God the power and the determination to do this. He did it in twenty-four hours.

In the morning when day came, the darkness disappeared. This was a special light. It was not the direct light from the rising sun. It was just light. [30]The Bible tells us that God is light.

Day 2
Genesis 1:6–8

To the right and to the left, ahead and behind, there was nothing but water. Looking upward something was missing. There was no sky, no clouds, no blue, no horizon, and maybe, no air to breathe.

"And God said, Let there be an expanse in the midst of the waters, and let it separate the waters from the waters." What is the expanse? The expanse is the atmosphere, the air surrounding the earth. Ninety-nine per cent of the air is composed of two gases: nitrogen and oxygen. Without these gases in the atmosphere no life could live on the earth.

"And God made the expanse and separated the waters which were under the expanse from the waters which were above the expanse, and it was so." There is water vapor in the atmosphere. Clouds form from water vapor that has risen from the earth. When the heavens send rain, this rain is for the earth. The earth receives the rain that the heavens send.

[31]God told Job that He could number the clouds, tip over the water jars of heaven, and send forth the lightning.

"And God called the expanse Heaven, And there was evening and there was morning, a second day."

Day 3
Genesis 1:9–13

God's next step was to prepare the earth so that life could grow. God knew that for the plant life to grow, He needed to gather the waters together into one place, so that the dry land could appear.

"And God said, Let the waters under the heavens be gathered together into one place, and let the dry land appear; and it was so. And God called the dry land Earth, and the gathering together of the waters He called Seas; and God saw that it was good."

[32]God simply gathered the waters to the place that He established for them. He set their borders so they could not turn back to cover the earth. [33]This allowed the land that was originally created by Him to reappear.

The angels who served God and remained with God were able to see the high mountains and the valleys that had been hidden under the waters.

God was busy on the third day. After He gathered the waters to one place and let the dry land appear, He did something else. He spoke again.

"**And God said, Let the earth sprout grass, herbs yielding seed, and fruit trees bearing fruit according to their kind with their seed in them upon the earth; and it was so. And the earth brought forth grass, herbs yielding seed according to their kind, and trees bearing fruit with their seed in them according to their kind.**"

Each plant began to grow according to their kind. "According to their kind" is a very important phrase. It means that the grass grew more grass that was exactly the same as the first plant. One plant could have many seeds. When those seeds fell into the ground, died, sprouted, then grew to maturity, they looked exactly the same as the plant that produced the seed. The same thing happened with the herbs (including vegetables) and the trees. God did not mix things up. The earth was important to Him, and what He spoke was what came forth.

The Bible does not tell us what kind of plants came forth but we know that Genesis 2:8-9 says that, "**Jehovah God planted a garden in Eden...and out of the ground Jehovah God caused to grow every tree that is pleasant to the sight and good for food.**" This "garden in Eden" was on the restored earth. It had come forth from God's speaking!

The dry land that appeared was clothed with a beautiful covering of many kinds of plants. These plants had all that they needed to grow and to multiply.

"And God saw that it was good. And there was evening and there was morning, a third day."

Carefully crack open a walnut shell and look at the way the seed is protected inside the shell. You will see a protective covering over the seed to keep it from moving around inside the shell. The design is amazing. If a walnut shell drops to the ground in autumn, God has a special way of caring for the seed within the shell. He provides the rich soil, the rain, the gentle breezes, and the warm sunshine. In time, the seed will grow roots and shoot upward, first as a sprout and then a sapling. Its trunk will get thicker and it will grow taller. Eventually it will blossom and produce more walnut seeds.

Psalm 56:9b – "This I know that God is for me."

Day 4
Genesis 1:14–19

The sun, the moon, and the stars were part of God's original creation. However, the shining of the light that came forth on the first day was not the shining of the sun, the moon, or the stars. On the fourth day God spoke, and the shining of the light-bearers was brought back into function.

"And God said, Let there be light-bearers in the expanse of heaven to separate the day from the night, and let them be for signs and for seasons and for days and years; And let them be light-bearers in the expanse of heaven to give light on the earth; and it was so."

The earth is tilted on its axis as it rotates around the sun. This slight tilt of the earth makes it possible for most parts of the earth to experience the seasons gradually changing from one season to the next.

In the northern hemisphere, the sun appears to be very close to the earth from late November to late January. In the morning, the colorful sunrise extends almost to the north. The midday sun does not go very high in the sky, and in the afternoon when you walk toward the south, the sun is so low that it shines right in your eyes. During this time, the hours of daylight get shorter and the evenings get colder. Why is this?

At this time of the year the northern hemisphere is tilted away from the sun.

God knows all the secrets in the universe.
These secrets show His glory. Today He shares
these secrets with us.

A snowflake is one of these secrets. It is impossible to count how many snowflakes are in this picture. Yet each snowflake starts as a tiny ice crystal that collides with a molecule or molecules of water vapour when the outside temperature in the cloud is within a certain range. On the way to earth these little snowflakes may bond with other snowflakes. When they finally arrive on a tree or on the ground each one is unique in its size and shape.

Psalm 147:16 – "He gives snow like wool;
He scatters frost like ashes."

"And God made the two great light-bearers, the greater light-bearer to rule the day and the lesser light-bearer to rule the night, and the stars."

The greater light-bearer is the sun, and the lesser light-bearer is the moon. Every day the earth makes one complete rotation on its own axis. As it rotates, the sun shines on a certain part of the earth, and the moon, following its own orbit, with the same side always facing the earth, reflects the sun, where it is seen on the earth. [34]The sun rules when it shines onto earth and the moon rules when it reflects the sun onto earth. Every day it takes the moon just under twenty-four hours to complete its orbit.

The moon, because it is much closer to the earth, has the greatest effect on tides. As the moon revolves around the earth, it causes the earth to have a slight bulge in the area closest to the equator. When the sun, the earth, and the moon are aligned, the gravitational pull of the sun and the moon work together to create the highest tides.

Long ago, the moon, the sun, and the stars were used to track time, determine location, and measure distance.

Morning and evening would mark one day. Every twenty-nine days, the eight distinct phases of the moon repeated. In the first phase, the new moon was somewhat hidden, but when the second phase was seen in the heavens, it became the marker for a new beginning. If someone wanted to track time, God had provided them with a way.

In ancient times at night, when the sailors were surrounded by water, they looked to the constellations and the moon to keep them on course. The North Star (called Polaris) was a key star.

In the day, the position of the sun helped them to know approximately what time it was and to chart the direction they were sailing.

Without God's provision, it would have been very scary for sailors to set sail on the ocean or for people to walk long distances. When it was time to return to their homeland, they were able to find the way back using the moon, the stars, and the sun to guide them.

"And God set them in the expanse of heaven to give light on the earth And to rule over the day and over the night and to separate the light from the darkness, and God saw that it was good. And there was evening and there was morning, a fourth day."

On the fourth day, God restored the sun, the moon, and the stars. The earth has seasonal changes that repeat every year, phases of the moon that repeat every month, light and darkness that repeat every day, and changes in the tide that repeat every twelve hours.

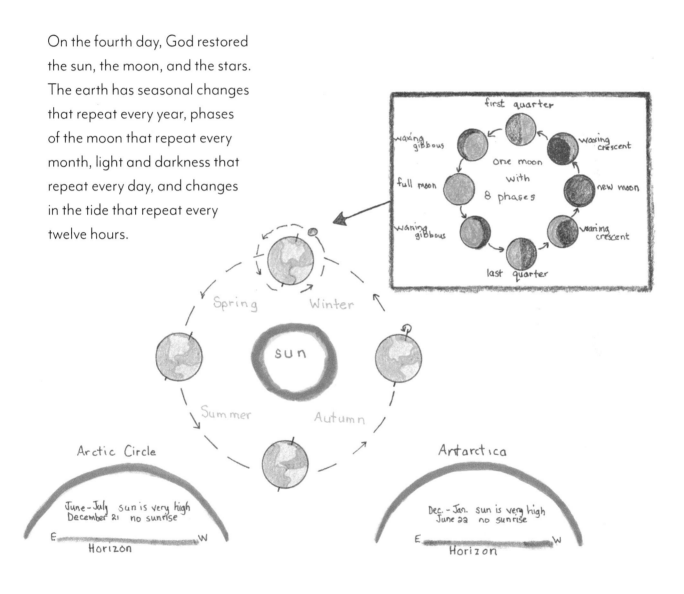

**When the sun goes below the horizon in one place,
it rises in another place on the earth.**

Day 5
Genesis 1:20–23

"And God said, Let the waters swarm with swarms of living animals, and let birds fly above the earth in the open expanse of heaven. And God created the great sea creatures and every living animal that moves, with which the waters swarmed, according to their kind, and every winged bird according to its kind; and God saw that it was good."

God was careful when He put the fish in the sea and the birds on the land and in the air. He designed each kind in a special way and provided them with a special habitat. The waters and the skies were full of living creatures.

In some parts of the Bay of Fundy, the tide reaches a height of 53 feet [10 meters]. Many lobsters live in this bay. As the tide waters flow in, they deliver a fresh supply of crabs, clams, mussels, starfish, and other small fish and sea plants. After the lobsters eat, they hide under the rocks and in the cracks in the sand while the waters flow back to the Atlantic Ocean. This is when they digest their meal and rest. Then as the tide reverses and flows back into the bay during the next six hours, the lobsters eat again. This cycle repeats itself every twelve hours and twenty-five minutes.

A beach provides a safe place where many animals and plants live. Small crabs usually live in a rock pool or under rocks. If they are frightened, they quickly run away and hide somewhere else. Acorn barnacles look like little hats firmly attached to rocks. Inside this barnacle is a tiny animal. When under water, it will send out six legs that act as a trap door to collect food.

Animals like sea lions, walruses, and baby seals relax in the warm sand and swim in the water. In the deeper waters of the ocean, big sea mammals like dolphins, porpoises, gray whales, and humpback whales can occasionally be seen.

At a certain time in their life cycle, adult salmon leave the ocean and follow the tide waters into a river such as the Fraser River **estuary**. They have no road map, only an inner sense that guides them. Some salmon do not travel far to arrive at their birthplace. Others travel a long distance even as far as the **headwaters** of a river. Their journey is dangerous.

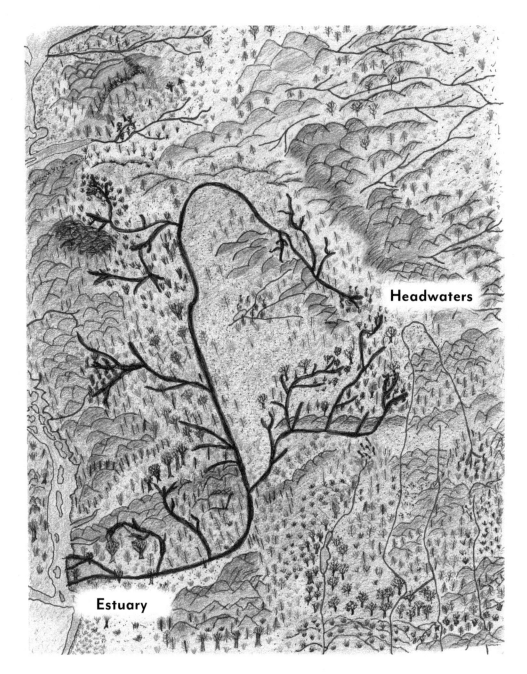

Headwaters

Estuary

When salmon reach their birthplace, they lay their eggs in gravel beds and then die. Later their eggs hatch, and tiny fish are seen everywhere. At the right time these young fish follow the same path back to the ocean. They will not have a "lead" fish who has traveled this path before. When they are mature adults, an inner sense will direct them to take the same journey their parents took to return to their birthplace, lay eggs, and die.

Penguins are birds. God designed their bodies in a special way. Their feathers keep them warm when it is very cold. When they swim, they look like they are flying under the water. They have a special brood pouch located close to their feet where they keep their egg warm. When the egg hatches, this pouch keeps the baby chick warm.

Father and mother penguin share the role of caring for the baby. As soon as the egg hatches, the mother will give the young chick to the father while she walks and swims a long distance searching for food to eat and to store in her stomach to feed their baby when she returns. The father does not eat while she is away. Every day he calls out to the mother. When the mother arrives back at the colony where there are many penguins standing around, she recognizes the father's call and goes to where he is standing with the chick. Immediately she regurgitates the food which she stored in her stomach and feeds the chick. The chick is transferred to her pouch, and the father leaves to take his turn to eat and bring back more food for the baby.

Some birds fly long distances. In the spring, the Arctic Tern flies north, sometimes as far as the Arctic. In the autumn, they fly the same way back to their wintering grounds, which may be the southern tip of South America. The round trip is twenty-five-thousand miles.

Birds like the eagle, hawk, and owl are birds of prey. Eagles have keen eyes and powerful wings. They glide in the air and when they see a small animal running on the forest floor or swimming in the stream, they dive quickly and capture it for their lunch. The hawk has a strong beak and large curved claws. Owls prefer to hunt at night. They have keen eyesight. Their ears detect the direction of a sound. This enables them to find their dinner even in the darkest nights.

From these examples we see God's love, His care, His attention to detail, and His wisdom, in protecting and providing for the needs of the birds who fly in the air, and for the creatures He placed on the earth and in the waters.

"And God blessed them, saying, Be fruitful and multiply, and fill the waters in the seas, and let the birds multiply on the earth. And there was evening and there was morning, a fifth day."

Day 6
Genesis 1:24–25

"And God said, Let the earth bring forth living animals according to their kind, cattle and creeping things and animals of the earth according to their kind; and it was so. And God made the animals of the earth according to their kind and the cattle according to their kind and everything that creeps on the ground according to its kind, and God saw that it was good."

More living animals were brought forth by God's speaking on the sixth day. Every animal that He made was according to its own kind. He did not randomly decide one day to create some sheep, some oxen, or perhaps a few lions and then perhaps the next day to add some creeping things such as snakes, lizards, and earthworms. It took Him one day to fill the earth with cattle, creeping things, and other animals.

Each animal had a special purpose in God's creation. He placed them in different places. Some lived in the desert; others in the forest; some made their home in holes in the ground and others were able to walk on rocky paths in the mountains.

God's wisdom is beyond our understanding. How could He possibly think of so many different animals and uniquely design each one the way He did?

For example, a camel is used by man to travel from one place to another. When God designed the camel, He knew that the camel would live in the desert and needed a way to store water and food for long journeys. Therefore, He gave some camels one hump and others two humps on their back.

God had another reason for placing animals on the earth. He knew that the man He was about to create would also have unique needs.

When the Plains Indians in North America killed a bison, they used the larger pieces of the hide to make tents. The smaller pieces were used to make clothing, harnesses for the dogs, ropes, string, and bowstrings. Some skins were cut so thin that the strands could be used to sew beads on their clothing. Nothing was wasted. The meat was cut into smaller pieces and dried in the sun, the fat was boiled down to make oil, and even the tendons were used. The Plains Indians were very thankful for this animal.

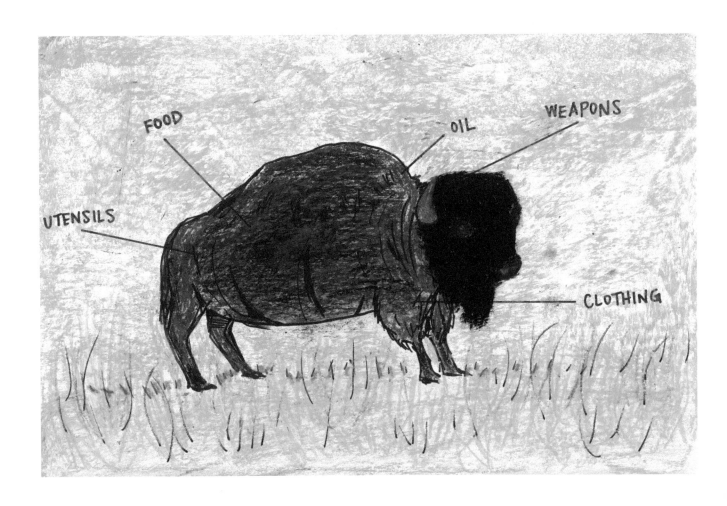

Bees are small. They need each other to survive. There is only one queen in a colony. This queen needs all the bees and all the bees need the queen. The queen bee is their mother. The bees all work together to take care of the needs of their colony. A colony may have one hundred male bees called drones. Some drones are soldiers who protect the queen and the colony. They can be seen walking near the door of the hive. A large colony may have twenty thousand or more female bees that are called workers. They are the bees that collect the nectar from the flowers and bring it to the colony. Other workers make a special substance and add it to the nectar to make royal jelly and honey. Some of the workers are nurse bees. They feed the larvae and baby bees. All the bees eat the honey that is stored in the honeycombs.

Bees need flowers so that they can collect nectar to bring to the hive. Berry bushes, fruit trees, and many other smaller plants need bees to pollinate their flowers so they can reproduce. Man is unable to grow honey. God in His wisdom knew how to take care of a need that bees, plants, and we have.

Every living thing created by God, including the blades of grass, the lilies in the fields, and the tiny sparrows, were important to God. God's unique design ensured that they had adequate food, water, and protection. Camouflage, hibernation, and migration are a few examples of His design.

God had spoken and the earth was ready. Everything was in perfect order again. There was fresh air, dry land, and water. Grass, herbs, and trees were moving in the wind. The sun, the moon, and the stars provided light during the day and the night. The gradual changes from winter, to spring, to summer, and then back to fall and winter were in place. There were fish in the water, birds in the air, and animals, big and small. Everything was growing and multiplying according to its own kind. The earth was peaceful and beautiful again.

Many years later, when God spoke to Job, He gave Job detailed information about things in the universe—little things, like snow and sprouts of grass. He spoke about the raven, hawk, eagle, and ostrich. He also mentioned the lioness, mountain goats, the wild and swift ass, the wild ox, and the horse. In chapter 40, God talked about *behemoth* (the hippopotamus), and in chapter 41, *leviathan* (the crocodile). After Job heard God speak these things, he said, **"I had heard of You by the hearing of the ear, But now my eye has seen You."**

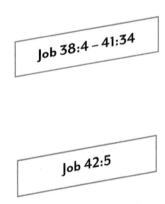

Job 38:4 – 41:34

Job 42:5

GOD HAD RESTORED THE DAMAGED
UNIVERSE; HOWEVER, AN
IMPORTANT PIECE WAS STILL MISSING.

GOD MADE MAN

Day 6 (cont.)
Genesis 1:26–28a, 31

**"And God said, Let Us make man in
Our image, according to Our likeness."**

Wow! Man was made in God's image,
and according to God's likeness,
"and"
even more amazing! God said,

"Let them have dominion over the fish of the sea and over the birds of heaven and over the cattle and over all the earth and over every creeping thing that creeps upon the earth."

God told man to fill the earth and subdue it, and to have authority over the fish of the sea, the birds of heaven, the cattle, and over every creeping thing that creeps upon the earth!

"And God created man in His own image; in the image of God He created him; male and female He created them. And God blessed them;...

And God saw everything that He had made, and indeed, it was very good. And there was evening and there was morning, the sixth day."

A LINGERING THOUGHT

The words in the Bible are a great anchor for us because they reveal "the facts."

In the first two verses of the Bible, God did not reveal any details to Moses. He gave him two facts: **"In the beginning God created the heavens and the earth,"** and **"But the earth became waste and emptiness, and darkness was on the surface of the deep."**

God had a special way of handling this matter. In the beginning, God knew, before He created the universe and the angels, what path Lucifer would take. Genesis 1:2a was the result of God's judgment on the parts of the universe damaged by Lucifer's footprints.

The heavens were created for the earth and the earth was created for man. [35]Man is God's unique possession and His personal treasure. In a very secret way, the Bible reveals that He took action to restore the earth, the heavenly light-bearers, the plant life, and the animal life so that planet Earth would be the best place for His people to live and know all that is in His heart. [36]It took Him six days to do this. What an amazing God He is!

**Ecclesiastes 3:14 – "I know that whatever God does,
it will be forever; nothing can be added to it, nor can anything
be taken from it. God has so done, that all would fear Him."**

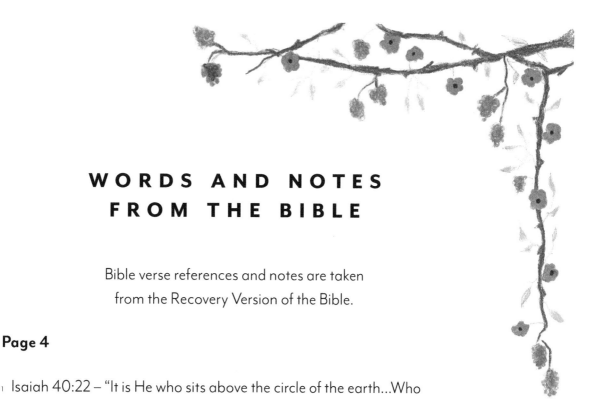

WORDS AND NOTES
FROM THE BIBLE

Bible verse references and notes are taken
from the Recovery Version of the Bible.

Page 4

1 Isaiah 40:22 – "It is He who sits above the circle of the earth...Who
stretches out the heavens."

Pages 5 to 8

2 Isaiah 45:18 – "For thus says Jehovah, Who created the heavens—He is
the God Who formed the earth and made it; He established it; He did not
create it waste, *But* He formed it to be inhabited: I am Jehovah and there is
no one else." (See also Hebrews 1:10, Hebrews 11:3.)

3 Isaiah 40:26 – "Lift up your eyes on high, And see who has created these
things, Who brings out their host by number; He calls all of them by name.
Through the greatness of His might and the strength of His power Not one
of them is missing."

4 Tectonic plates

5 Mariana trench

6 Job 10:13a – "But You have hidden these things in Your heart."

Pages 9 and 10

7 Ezekiel 28:13a
Note 13[1] clarifies that this Eden was located in the heavenlies.

8 Psalm 103:19-21 – "Jehovah has established His throne in the heavens, And His kingdom rules over all. Bless Jehovah, you His angels, Who are mighty in strength to perform His word, By obeying the voice of His word... You His ministers who execute His will."

9 Ezekiel 28:14
Note 14[4] shows how privileged the anointed cherub was. (See also Ezekiel 28:12b, 15a.)

10 Isaiah 14:12b – "O Daystar, son of the dawn!"
Note 12[1] [first part] highlights Lucifer at the "dawn" of the universe.

11 Luke 4:6b – "To You I will give all this authority and their glory, because to me it has been delivered, and to whomever I want I give it."
Note 6[1] [first part] unveils the scope of Lucifer's authority and glory.

Page 11

12 Isaiah 14:12-14
Note 13[1] and 13[2] reveal his intention. (Ezekiel 28:15b, 17a.)

13 I John 3:8 – "...the devil has sinned from the beginning."
Notes I John 3:8[3] and Leviticus 13:2[1] [middle of the paragraph] reveal the origin of sin; I John 1:1, note 1[2] defines "the beginning."

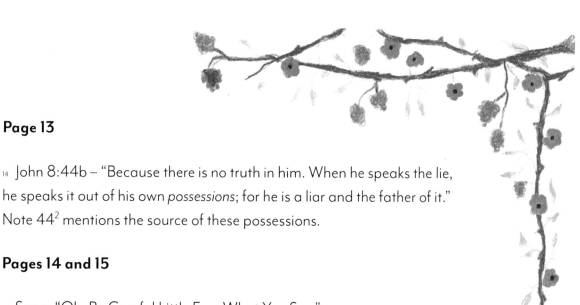

Page 13

14 John 8:44b – "Because there is no truth in him. When he speaks the lie, he speaks it out of his own *possessions*; for he is a liar and the father of it." Note 44[2] mentions the source of these possessions.

Pages 14 and 15

15 Song: "Oh, Be Careful Little Eyes What You See." https://www.hymnal.net/en/hymn/c/157

16 Song: "God's Word – Have I Hid in my Heart." https://www.hymnal.net/en/hymn/c/145

Pages 19 and 20

17 Colossians 1:20[5] and Hebrews 9:23[1] [second half of the note] indicate that the heavens and all things were defiled [contaminated] by the rebellion of Satan and the fallen angels.

18 Luke 10:18 – "And He said to them, I was watching Satan fall like lightning out of heaven." Note 18[1] Satan's judgment and its execution. (Ezekiel 28:16b)

19 Ephesians 6:12[2] – "spiritual *forces* of evil in the heavenlies." Note 12[2] describes who these forces are.

Page 21

20 Job 9:5-7 Note 5[1] suggests the timing of these events.

Pages 22 and 23

₂₁ Genesis 1:2a –
Note 2¹, 2³ and 2⁴ are crucial to understanding God's original creation [Genesis 1:1] and God's judgment on the universe [Genesis 1:2a]. (See Note 15¹ in Isaiah 14:15 for further understanding.)

Pages 24 and 25

₂₂ Ephesians 1:9 – "Making known to us the mystery of His will according to His good pleasure, which He purposed in Himself." (Refer to Note 9⁴ and Deuteronomy 10:14.)

₂₃ Numbers 23:19 – "God is not a man, that He should lie, Nor a son of man, that He should repent. Has He said, and will He not do it? Or has He spoken, and will He not establish it?"

₂₄ Isaiah 40:28 – "Do you not know, Or have you not heard, That the eternal God, Jehovah, The Creator of the ends of the earth, Does not faint and does not become weary? There is no searching out of His understanding."

₂₅ Psalm 104:5 – "He established the earth upon its foundations, So that it cannot be moved forever and ever."

₂₆ Hebrews 1:3b – "...upholding and bearing all things by the word of His power." (Refer to Note 3².)

₂₇ Colossians 1:16a, 17 – "Because in Him all things were created, in the heavens and on the earth, the visible and the invisible...all things have been created through Him and unto Him. And He is before all things, and all things cohere in Him." (Refer to Note 16⁵ and 17².)

Pages 26 and 27

28 Genesis 1:2b

29 Note Genesis 1:2^4 sentence beginning "The entire section from 1:2b—"

30 I John 1:5b – "God is light and in Him is no darkness at all."

Page 28

31 Job 38:35, 37 – "Can you send forth lightnings...Who can number the clouds by wisdom, Or who can tip over the water jars of heaven."

Page 30

32 Psalm 104:7-9 – "At Your rebuke they fled; At the voice of Your thunder they rushed away—The mountains rose, the valleys sank—to the place that you established for them. You set a border [for the water] that they may not pass over, that they may not turn back to cover the earth."

33 Nee, Watchman. *Collected Works of Watchman Nee.* Set One, Vol. 3. pp. 34-36.

Page 35

34 Psalm 136:8-9 – "The sun for ruling the day...The moon and the stars for ruling the night."

Page 49

35 Exodus 19:4b, 5b – "How I bore you on eagles' wings and brought you to Myself...you shall be My personal treasure...for all the earth is Mine."

36 Exodus 20:11 – "For in six days Jehovah made heaven and earth, the sea and all that is in them, and rested on the seventh day."

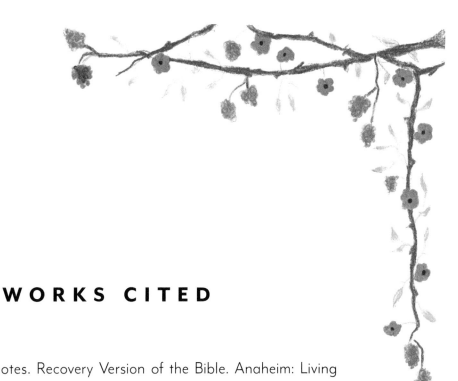

WORKS CITED

Lee, Witness. Footnotes. Recovery Version of the Bible. Anaheim: Living Stream Ministry, 2003.

_____. Life-Study of Genesis. Messages 1-3. Anaheim: Living Stream Ministry.

_____. The Collected Works of Witness Lee, Vol. 1 (1932-49). Anaheim: Living Stream Ministry, 2018. pp. 148-170 and pp. 327-328.

Nee, Watchman. "The Christian (1)." The Collected Works of Watchman Nee, Set 1: The Early Period, 1922-1934, Vol. 3. Anaheim: Living Stream Ministry, 1992. pp. 1-36.

Pember, G. H. Earth's Earliest Ages. Grand Rapids, Michigan: Kregel Publications, 1975. Chapters 1 and 2.

Songs: https://www.hymnal.net/

CPSIA information can be obtained
at www.ICGtesting.com
Printed in the USA
BVHW021628021120
592189BV00001B/1